Online Community Management

Grow and Develop an Active Audience on Social Media

Online Community Management

Grow and Develop an Active Audience on Social Media

Dr. Amy Jauman

National Institute for Social Media

ISBN: 978-1-946649-10-2

Special thanks to the following content reviewers from the National Institute for Social Media community. We appreciate your feedback and continued support!

- Jennifer Radke, SMS
- Kimberly Behzadi, MBA, SMS
- Crystal Lindsey, MBA
- Forrest Flinn, SMS, PHR/SHRM-CP
- Kellyn Kawaguchi
- Teri Kojetin
- Heather Rule
- Margaret Stewart, SMS

What is the National Institute for Social Media (NISM)?

The National Institute for Social Media (NISM) is an organization dedicated to social media certification and education for professional social media practitioners. In partnership with organizations and lifelong learning enthusiasts, they've created a community for professional development and set the standards for social media education, assessment and certification, and consulting. NISM provides the foremost Social Media Strategy (SMS) certification exam in the US, which allows social media professionals to obtain a recognized professional standard in this continually developing field.

Who's the author?

Dr. Amy Jauman is a certified Social Media Strategist and lead instructor at the National Institute for Social Media. She is a social media consultant, writer and professor and her formal education includes a master's degree in experiential education, so you'll find plenty of real-world application prompts. She also has a doctorate in organization development, so there's a lot of information about how to work with people in a variety of business environments. Her interest in helping people prepare for and pass the SMS certification exam was piqued in 2011 when she began looking for ways she could establish her credibility in social media.

Dr. Jauman discovered that many of her peers working in social media and students venturing out as marketing professionals had the same need for social media credentials that accurately represented their knowledge and experience. When presented with the chance to write these books and provide students and professionals with a practical guide to the six content domains covered in the SMS certification exam, she jumped at the opportunity.

Who should read this book?

There are likely three groups of people who would benefit most from reading this book, although it is of value to anyone with an interest in fostering active online communities via their social media channels.

Anyone prepping to take the SMS certification exam. If you're thinking about taking the SMS exam, you've probably discovered that community management is one of six content domains covered.. Whether or not you're familiar with the concept of community management, this book can be a great way to quickly and easily check out what's covered on the exam. It can also help you identify areas you might want to learn more about before your exam.

Anyone considering a role that is entirely or in part associated with managing online communities. It's possible that the depth and breadth of the SMS certification exam doesn't interest you. If you're more interested in one area of social media – working exclusively in community management as opposed to the broader role of being a certified social media strategist – this book can provide you with insights specific to your area of interest. One of the reasons we transitioned from a single, large textbook to six smaller books was to connect with the social media professionals interested in joining our community through their expertise in one or two of the content domains.

Anyone considering hiring an expert in community management. It's possible that you aren't even interested in social media strategy or certification – but you're smart enough to know it's important. This book can act as a great guide for any leader in any industry considering adding a social media community manager to the team.

However you're connected to the National Institute for Social Media (NISM) and whatever you'd like to learn from this book, we invite you to connect with us. Find us on Facebook at facebook.com/NISMPulse, Twitter @NISMPulse or any of the sites listed at nismonline.org.

The National Institute for Social Media
Code of Ethics

The Code of Ethics is intended to reflect the standards and behavior that National Institute for Social Media ("NISM") certified practitioners and program applicants expect of each other as they perform their duties and that reaffirm the value of holding an NISM credential. The purpose of the Code of Ethics is to ensure public confidence in the integrity and service of NISM-certified professionals while performing their duties.

The Code of Ethics identifies the types of circumstances that may compromise the reliability of NISM's ability to establish, or certify, a certificate holder's or program applicant's ability to perform the essential tasks of the vocation with at least minimal competency. For purposes of this Code of Ethics, "essential tasks" are defined as the general vocational duties that are expected to be performed by NISM-certified professionals. "Minimal competency" is defined as the ability to perform the essential tasks effectively, with minimal supervision.

NISM does not monitor on-the-job behavior or actions. Adherence to these ethical standards is expected from all certificate holders and applicants. Any violation may be subject to removal of his or her certified status.

All NISM certificate holders and applicants are expected to adhere to the following standards of professional conduct and ethics:

1. We represent ourselves truthfully, honestly, and to the best of our abilities throughout the entire certification process, and in performance of the essential tasks described in section 3 of the candidate handbook.

2. We adhere to all exam site rules, making no attempt to complete an exam dishonestly or to assist any other person in doing so.
3. We protect proprietary or confidential information that has been entrusted to us as if it were our own.
4. We state only what we know to be true, and are clear about opinions and assumptions vs. facts.
5. We are transparent about who we are, and whom or what we represent online.
6. We take ownership of our online activities, the content we have created, and any missteps we have made along the way.
7. We uphold the policies, rules, regulations and laws that govern our activities.
8. We report unethical or illegal conduct to appropriate authorities.

Contents

Introduction

Community Management

*"You can never go wrong by investing in communities
and the human beings within them."*

- Pam Moore (@pammktgnut)

C ommunity management supports the two-way online communication between an organization and its customers. A strong, well-managed community is active, and there's a free flow of ideas between the community manager and consumers – and even between current and potential customers. The community manager acts as a professional representative for the organization by asking questions, responding to comments and gathering feedback that eventually leads to an improved product and overall better experience for the customer.

In addition to connecting and talking to customers, community management also includes advocating for a brand through a social persona. A community manager's goal is to increase awareness of the organization, which happens naturally through online conversations but can be even more effective with careful planning. Good community managers keep their organization front of mind, of course, but they seek to forge genuine connections with consumers.

The NISM Candidate Handbook describes community management in part as *"the process of ensuring that the two-way online communication between the organization and its customers/stakeholders always flows smoothly. The manager serves as a professional representative for the organization's products or services, while simultaneously gathering feedback for further development of products or services for evaluation."* As you can see, the focus of this role is on the customer. The goal for the community manager is to facilitate two-way conversations that lead to idea sharing and customer appreciation that will ultimately fuel continuous improvement of the organization and brand loyalty from the customer.

In addition to the tactical approaches for encouraging online engagement that community managers are typically eager to read about, we're going to talk about what good community management looks like at a strategic level.

The book has four primary sections:

- **Create Connections**

  A common challenge for community managers – especially if community management is just one of many hats they wear – is getting started. After all, you can prepare to be the perfect conversation partner, but if no one is there to hear your message, your work is in vain. There are a few core requirements for building a community – a good product, consumers who trust you, time to foster relationships – that may or may not be easy for your organization, but wherever you are in your brand development, there are some tactics you can employ to increase your reach.

- **Create the Right Content**

  Content is explored in greater detail in the NISM book *Marketing & Communications: The Right Social Media Content at the Right Time.* However, we will briefly discuss the importance of sharing information that will keep community members engaged – content and opportunities that serve them so they are willing to support you.

- **Give More than You Receive**

    As brand representatives, it's easy to fall into the trap of only talking about yourself. You want to share what *you* have to offer, what *you're* working on, and even how *you* can solve your customer's greatest challenges. This typically comes from a good place. You believe in what your organization has to offer to such an overwhelming degree, you can't stop talking about it. But because so many businesses think that way, social media is filled with people talking about themselves. Commenting on posts, answering questions, and listening to what your customers are saying without selling are both beneficial to your brand and product development as well as your reputation for being genuinely interested in the success of your community.

- **Make the Best of Bad Situations**

    There is a strong temptation to talk about the familiar topic of your brand because it keeps the conversation under control. The difficulty with two-way conversations is that you never know what your customer is going to say – and for some people that thought is terrifying. We'll talk about how community managers can develop a crisis response plan that will decrease the anxiety associated with the unknown and simultaneously increase the efficiency and effectiveness of your team members responding to customers online.

Understanding why you're completing various tasks as a community manager – the strategy behind your work – is important to your success and a critical component assessed on the SMS certification exam. But don't worry – we know that specific techniques are important, too, and we have plenty of suggestions for you. In fact, reading further in the description of community management in the NISM Candidate Handbook, you will see the exam covers some tactical approaches.

"Candidates will be measured on their understanding of essential tasks within this competency domain. The community management domain consists of frequently reaching out and engaging with your audience, fostering a sense of excitement about the organization within the social space, and reacting quickly and appropriately to unexpected situations. Methods for making connections between members of a community, reading, commenting and responding to the content, comments, or questions of community members, and recognizing the accomplishments of those in an organization's network are also assessed. Moreover, candidates are tested on their capacity to interpret why a customer or client is upset and find a solution, while also showing understanding of internal networking techniques – knowing who to talk to when a customer has a question or need."

Other content domains on the SMS exam – project management, strategic planning, compliance and governance – do focus more on strategic concepts. As a social media professional, it's important not to get caught in the weeds of tactical work. However, in cases like community management, we'll discover a lot of value in the carefully planned and managed tactics.

NISM 2016 Social Media Job Study

54.5% of participants ranked planning and goal setting as a task of high importance. This is an increase of 34.3% from the 2012 study.

25.9% of those surveyed spend more than 10 hours each week on project management tasks.

Each content domain increased in importance from 2012 to 2016.

The most important task within Marketing & Communications was

Branding

66.5% identified it as highly important.

The NISM 2016 Social Media Job Study

43 states.
20 industries.
533 men and women.
Managers, employees and consultants.

68.8% of participants cited acting appropriately without direction as highly important. It was perceived as important in 2012 as well, but only 43.6% chose **highly important.**

Responding to comments increased from low to high importance between 2012 and 2016.

#NISM2016JS

Content domains explored through the job study are the same as the SMS exam.
Project Management
Governance & Compliance
Marketing & Communications
Research & Analysis
Strategic Planning
Community

The value of 2-way communication with customers increased from medium to high importance.

www.nismonline.org

Part One
Creating Connections

Chapter 1

NISM Job Study Results

In the 2016 NISM Social Media Job Study, designed to understand the key responsibilities of social media strategists, we asked about the prevalence and importance of community management. Community management was described to survey participants as:

"Built around a foundation of quality content, community management is the process of ensuring that the two-way online communication between the organization and its customers/stakeholders always flows smoothly. The manager serves as a professional representative for the organization's products or services, while simultaneously gathering feedback for further development of products or services for evaluation."

The survey questions focused on the following five aspects of community management:

- Reading and responding to customer posts
- Having two-way conversations with customers on social media
- Finding ways to frequently reach out and engage with your audience
- Apologizing if you do something that offends someone, admitting your mistakes and moving on
- Recognizing accomplishments of those in your network

In the first social media job study conducted by NISM in 2012, community management was ranked as highly important. Comparing the 2012 and 2016 results, survey participants again ranked each of the five categories as very important. Two notable results from the survey were:

- The perceived importance of two-way conversations with customers was given medium importance by the largest percentage of survey participants in 2012 (35.1%) whereas the largest group in 2016 (53.3%) ranked it as highly important.
- In each of the five categories, the percentage of people who ranked the task as highly important increased – in some cases significantly.

Survey participants were given the opportunity to share additional thoughts about the importance of community management. Some of their additional feedback included comments related to:

- The importance of curating content for customers
- Significance of content that informs, educates and inspires
- The value of engagement
- The power of connecting with influencers

When we explored the varying value of importance expressed by our survey participants, some specific questions arose:

- What are some of the obstacles that prevent organizations, marketers and social media professionals from engaging in communities in a meaningful way?
- What techniques can community managers use to make their jobs easier and more effective?
- What are the best ways and the best content to foster a healthy online community?

These questions are examples of how social media professionals might explore and further understand the role of a community manager. NISM, and particularly the SMS certification exam, focuses on community management in general and is not industry or organization specific.

We will address these issues in the following sections of this book, to help you understand what you can do to be an effective community manager. We will explore how you can:

- Frequently reach out and engage with your audience
- Foster a sense of excitement about the company within the social space
- React quickly and appropriately to unexpected situations
- Make connections between others as appropriate
- Interpret why a customer is angry and how to find a solution
- Read, comment, and respond to the content or comments of your customers
- Recognize accomplishments of those in your network
- Apologize if you do something that offends someone, admit your mistakes, and move on
- Empathize with your audience, looking beyond the words into the greater context within which a person is writing
- Have two-way conversations with customers on social media platforms
- Network within your company, so you know who to talk to when a customer has a question or need

Chapter 2

Two-Way Communication

An active online community has information constantly moving in multiple directions. The community manager and members post content and everyone within the community is encouraged to respond with their own unique contribution. Whatever the topic, the power of an online community is in the ability for many people to rally around a shared bond and feel empowered to contribute.

Content posted by the community manager may vary greatly depending on the purpose and design of the group. An online community associated with an organization is likely to post some or all of the following components supplied by the organization:

- Company newsletter information
- Events hosted by or associated with the organization, industry, or community
- Deals or opportunities for customers/fans
- Posts from the organization's blog or related industry posts

- Articles related to the organization or industry
- Content from company social media channels

Creative community managers also have the opportunity to kick engagement up a notch by inviting community members to contribute, such as:

- Inviting community members to write blog posts
- Launching simple opinion polls, then encouraging members to participate in the poll and comment on the topic being discussed

Encouraged by the community manager or not, individual members of an online community may contribute:

- Product feedback (positive and negative)
- Concerns or suggestions related to the organization, industry, or a current event

No matter what combination of these techniques works for your individual organization, one thing is true: you need active community members to make the conversations interesting. Once the conversations are going, your community will grow naturally. Active members will invite others, people will share content, and you'll appear in more searches as you solve more and more problems and more people respond. In an online community, the bigger you are, the more opportunities you'll have to grow – often naturally and with very little effort. But how do you get started?

Social Media Personas

Social media professionals will often create a social media persona they associate with the organization. The persona becomes who the community hears from – the face of the organization. There are three types of personas typically used: personal, corporate, and response community personas. When acting as any of the personas, the community manager uses their skills to best represent the organization and connect with the consumers.

Personal Persona

In some cases, it's best for the community manager to post as themselves. This is the most personal approach and is typically received well. In small communities, this might be easier to implement since the personal persona may very well be one person. In larger organizations, it can be more challenging to maintain consistency in messaging. In these cases, it's critical to have a communications guide and an individual monitoring communications.

Corporate/Brand Persona

Corporate or brand personas are a single resource who speaks for the organization. The most notable difference between personal and corporate personas is that corporate personas rarely connect on a personal level with their community. A benefit of a corporate persona is that any turnover within the organization will go unnoticed in the community. With a robust communications plan, the corporate persona won't change.

Response Community Persona

Banks, cable companies, restaurant chains, and other businesses that have a high volume of communication on social media platforms use a hybrid version of personal and corporate personas called a response community persona. All of the responses come from one corporate account, but each employee retains their own voice and often includes their name or initials within the communication. Employees are encouraged to include their personality in their responses. (Chapter 8 has several examples of response community posts.)

Whatever persona you choose for your organization, it's important to consider what is feasible for your organization and what you can do to ensure consistent messaging.

Pinned Tweet

ComcastCares @comcastcares · 6h
Most customers should see their TV service back up and running. We appreciate your patience while we worked to resolve.

Determining Your Voice

Community managers are responsible for encouraging conversations online. There are several different ways personas can be used to support an organization, and the community manager needs to be able to move seamlessly between them. Whether a personal, corporate, or response community persona is required, the community manager should follow the expectations set in the style guide and remain consistent.

XFINITY @XFINITY · Nov 27
We're opening our XFINITY #WiFi public hotspots nationwide starting at 6am #CyberMonday! Learn more: xfin.tv/2gguLgw

XFINITY WIFI
FREE ACCESS FOR EVERYONE
ON CYBER MONDAY

In some cases, efficient community management will involve a broadcast message, intended to inform as many people as possible of an important message. The tone would be clear and informative. The example from Comcast is a pinned tweet – sure to reach anyone who visits their Twitter profile – and is direct and to-the-point. The voice is consistent with other ComcastCares messaging focused on resolving customer issues, yet distinctly different from their parent Twitter account. xFinity messages are much lighter, focusing on entertainment and the benefits of internet and cable connectivity.

In other cases, a more individualized response is best. In the sample Facebook post below, a Wells Fargo community manager connected with a customer individually, addressed her by name, shared specific directions, and signed off with their name. In this case, the response was to a specific customer concern and required individualized attention both to ensure a resolution and to assure the community that the institution responds to customer concerns quickly and in a meaningful way.

Wells Fargo ✔ Hello, Karen. I'd like the opportunity to review your payment concerns. Without sharing account numbers, please send a private message with your best contact number, mailing address, and any additional details. Thank you. ~Cory

Like · Reply · ◎ 5 · September 30 at 2:17pm

Your organization will use one voice that will vary by situation but remain consistent throughout the organization's communications. One way to think of this is by considering how you speak in your personal life. Sometimes you're happy, angry, or confused, so your messages might change slightly, but you'll use similar words and phrases and you'll never lose your accent. Small changes based on the situation are normal, and you still sound like you.

Chapter 2 Discussion

1. What opportunities do you currently have to facilitate two-way conversations in your community? List platforms and topics.

2. Look at communities similar to (i.e., competitors) or related to your community. What topics engage their community members in conversation?

3. As a customer, when have you experienced the different kinds of conversations described in in this chapter?

4. Which persona type is best for your community and why?

Chapter 3

Gaining Active Community Members

One of the biggest challenges community managers are faced with is *how* to build their community. It isn't as simple as buying followers or running a contest that boosts the size of your subscriber list. That's a great way to build your *audience*. Your community is different – they are more active and invested in your success. Both are important, however. Here is a little more about the difference between the two.

Audience versus Community

An *audience* for your message includes anyone interested in receiving the information you are sharing. A marketer might be wise to invest a great deal of time and effort into building and maintaining the right audience because the audience members are likely to buy their products and even refer their friends. The role of an audience member doesn't include contributing to the development of the community. They might have feedback or suggestions – and in that way they do participate in a two-way conversation. But they are primarily interested in receiving what is being offered.

A *community* for your message, on the other hand, involves the right people interested in contributing to the continued success of your organization. These are individuals who are so invested in the work you're doing, they respond to your messages, share posts and act on behalf of the organization when the opportunity arises.

What might make a person become more invested in your community than another? Social media professionals sometimes express frustration with their internal or external online community when there is a lack of participation online, but those feelings won't help build an active community. What will help is attempting to understand the main reason people choose not to engage with your message: feeling like their time is well-spent.

People only have so much time, so if the content they're seeing and the conversations they're engaged in aren't valuable to them, they are unlikely to remain engaged. Many individuals are balancing professional and family commitments on top of learning from and contributing to communities. It's a lot to keep track of, so anything that isn't making their life better is at risk of getting cut. Author Rick Warren was quoted as saying,

"Time is your most precious gift because you only have a set amount of it. You can make more money, but you can't make more time. When you give someone your time, you are giving them a portion of your life that you'll never get back. Your time is your life. That is why the greatest gift you can give someone is your time."

People have so many options for communities they can participate in and will be motivated by multiple factors to join yours. A major factor is, of course, the topic, but they will also value the time that they spend with you and the other contributing members. Once you find the *right* people who consider engaging with your online community valuable, make sure the content and conversations in your community are a worthwhile investment of their time.

Real-Time Marketing (RTM) Opportunities

Who's already talking about your business or industry? What conversations are individuals, groups, or businesses already having about the work you're doing? Too often marketers think they have to *start* engaging conversations, when the best route is often to join one that's already happening!

There are several definitions of real-time marketing (RTM) used regularly – and they all have their merits. Some define RTM as responding to customer needs as immediately as possible – kind of like the ultimate version of social listening. Others define it as a way to run a marketing campaign by responding to what's happening in the moment instead of creating a plan in advance.

For the purposes of community building, we're going to consider a very small part of the RTM techniques Chris Kerns describes in his book *Trendology: Building an Advantage through Data-Driven Real-Time Marketing*. Kerns doesn't promote easy wins and quick fixes, but if you're interested in a structured approach to analyzing trends related to your business, the book is a must-read. The component we're going to look at for community building is the four categories he created for spotting opportunities to connect with people interested in your industry.

Kerns' idea is that, in our busy world, events all fall into one of four categories. Below is a brief description of each.

> **Planned Events:** For our purposes, we'll think of these as significant events for which we know the details – where, when, and why people interested in our topic are getting together, what they're hoping to accomplish, and the topics they're likely to discuss online. An example of this might be a large, annual fundraiser, a scheduled product launch, or an event like the Super Bowl.
>
> You can prepare for these events by identifying the hashtag that will be used, the people who will be in attendance who have a strong online presence, and relevant information that's likely to come up. Since you have so many details, you may even find opportunities to connect and have conversations before the actual event.

Watchlist Events: These are slightly less predictable events, but we still know they'll happen and we know they'll generate a lot of conversations online. If you think about recent events in the news, how often is the public watching and waiting for something to happen? There might be research that's generating excitement, even though the final results haven't been announced. A popular TV show might be approaching a critical episode. Something in nature – animals, a storm, or some kind of natural wonder – might be under close scrutiny. Watchlist events are valuable because they captivate people to such an extent that they join the conversation – often by contributing, but also by checking in, following hashtags, and scheduling alerts. There is

> Each of these four categories has one thing in common: The topics bring people together.

often an engaged audience and you can join the conversation.

Everyday Events: This isn't any more complicated than it sounds! If you look around, you'll soon spot everyday events – small-scale happenings, hashtags, and heroes. If you have a brick-and-mortar shop that also ships nationally, you'll draw two unique sets of traffic: online shoppers from around the country and your neighbors who live within a 20-mile radius of your store. Everyday events can appeal to both, but the most obvious match is the local shopper! Consider a local chocolatier who's selling holiday gifts packaged in the colors the local football teams wear. If the big homecoming dance is just around the corner, it's likely an event the neighborhood is talking about and a relevant product can usher you into the spotlight.

Opportunistic Events: This kind of event might be the most challenging to capitalize on because it is the most difficult to plan for, but can also yield some of the best results. These are the events that we couldn't have seen coming, but because we're well-researched and well-prepared marketers, we can respond quickly and join the conversation. For example, if everyone on the internet is excitedly talking about wildlife rescue workers creating a habitat for an endangered species of bird nesting on the roof of a building in New York, your home security system company might chime in. You might choose to inspire others by making a donation and encouraging others to do the same, reminding them of the importance of a safe home. Or you might join the hashtag with a clever line such as:

Do they need a security system? We could talk to our R&D team about what we could do for a nest. #savetheNYCbirds

The key to making the most of opportunistic events is responding quickly and in a way that makes you stand out.

Oreo capitalized on a power outage during the 2013 Super Bowl and launched this perfect response: "Power out? No problem" and then shared an image of the classic Oreo cookie with the caption, "You can still dunk in the dark."

The day after the Super Bowl, *Forbes* Staff Writer Jennifer Rooney wrote,

Last night, Oreo hit it big with a real-time marketing effort that became the talk--and tweet--of the Super Bowl. The "you can still dunk in the dark" tweet was retweeted almost 15,000 times. Oreo's Twitter following, meanwhile, increased by about 8,000. The blackout post garnered nearly 20,000 likes on Facebook. And Oreo went from having 2,000 Instagram followers pre-game to 36,000, with more than 16,000 pictures submitted by consumers as votes for "Cookie" or "Creme," tying to their Super Bowl ad-spurred seven-week contest for the best part of the Oreo, a Mondelez International brand.

As you can see in the *Forbes* summary, Oreo saw immediate growth on multiple social media platforms – undeniably because of the dunk-in-the-dark tweet. But the Forbes article goes on to explain that it wasn't just luck; it was a classic example of real-time marketing executed perfectly. They recognized the Super Bowl as a great opportunity, their marketing team was together and ready to make the most of every opportunity and – though they never could have anticipated a blackout – they were ready to respond creatively to whatever happened at this highly publicized, live event.

Each of these four categories has one thing in common: The topics bring people together. The extent to which community members are committed to the conversation, the popularity of the topic, reach, and duration will vary for every individual opportunity, but the opportunity remains the same. Instead of casting your information out into the world with limited direction and purpose, you have the opportunity to deliver – and potentially land – information about your community with a group of people who are already interested in and talking about your topic.

To make the most of these opportunities, brainstorm with your team or trusted peers. Follow true brainstorming practices – don't limit your ideas. Capture everything that comes to mind, even if it sounds ridiculous. You never know which idea will spark the perfect approach.

Create Your RTM Plan

1. Consider each of the four categories and list every possible idea you can come up with.

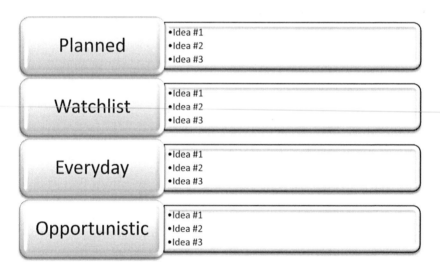

2. Once you feel you've shared all of the best possible ideas, choose which ones you know you can complete with the time and resources you have. This will be dependent on your resources, and there's no point in committing to more than you can actually do! Ideas you

love but can't start quite yet can always be added to a follow-up list for a future date.

3. Prepare to join each conversation by completing the following research:

   a. Identify the related hashtags.

   b. Determine what platforms will be the most active (typically similar events in the past or where the topic has the largest following are the best indicators).

   c. Identify personas who have a large following who are likely to be present. If possible, connect with them in advance in a meaningful way.

   d. Create a calendar that will allow you to maximize your participation (i.e., schedule small, regular check-ins if the event takes place over time or block the specific event time if it is primarily a one-time occurrence).

   e. As much as possible, compile statistics, quotes, related articles created by your team, etc. so they are fresh in your mind and ready to share.

When you join these conversations, your focus will be contributing to meaningful content. Don't push your product or share content about potential savings. Represent your business well by adding value to the topic.

Using RTM to Build Community

One of the primary benefits of working with communities in real time is that at the moment you're sharing content, you have good reason to believe your audience is interested in what you have to say. And in addition to the audience you typically connect with, there's a good chance you'll connect with some people who have never even heard of your brand. For example, if a celebrity is injured while riding a bicycle and your community is focused on bike safety, there will be a bump – however brief – in discussion around safe bicycling practices. During that bump, you'll have the opportunity to:

- Gain exposure for your product by joining active conversation with high-profile people and organizations
- Uncover and connect with groups who share common interests
- Identify new community members possibly interested in supporting your community's goals
- Find new audience members who have never heard of your product

Tapping into Groups

Joining groups that are already interested in what you're offering is an efficient way to find potential community members. Instead of having to generate interest and then connect with people, you simply join a conversation where interest has already been expressed.

Depending on the platform, groups form and can be found in different ways. For any platform, you have to begin by identifying the keywords or phrases that will help you connect with the right people. Techniques for identifying keywords are discussed in several of the NISM textbooks, but if you haven't run across the suggestions listed yet or if you just need a refresher, here's an excerpt from NISM's 2012 textbook that can help you can get started.

Keyword Selection

When selecting keywords, consider the following:

a. *Think like your customer, and choose words that they would use in search queries to find the products and services you offer.*

b. *Keywords should be specific phrases. If your keywords are too specific, you may not reach a large enough audience to get the impact you desire. Your keywords have to target those highly relevant searches, but also appeal to a substantial audience.*

c. *Single-word keywords are generally too broad; therefore, multiple-word keywords are generally better. You may wish to try long-tail keywords to improve search results rankings or the quality of visitors coming to your site.*

d. *Create groups of keywords for all of your unique products and services. According to Google, anywhere from five to 20 words or phrases per group is a good starting point, but the keywords group may be larger.*

Remember that the goal for keywords is to drive the right type of people to your website. For example, if your site provides product comparisons and makes money through advertising revenue, then having the term "comparison" or "compare" in your keywords is probably a good choice. If you want customers who are ready to buy, then those terms in your keywords might not be a good choice.

Long-Tail Keywords

Long-tail keywords are keyword phrases that are made up of more words. If your keyword has less words, there is a greater chance that it will match search queries. Though that may seem like a good thing, this means there is less likelihood that the keyword search will lead to a highly relevant match, and there will be more competition for search rankings. For example, if you use the keyword "shoes," you might match queries looking for athletic shoes, shoe repair, and horse shoes. If you have more words in your keyword phrase, you will have less competition, and match more relevant queries. Many organizations use two- to four-word keywords. There is typically still a lot of competition for keyword phrases of that length. With this in mind, you should also consider using long-tail keywords — keywords with an even greater number of words in the keyword phrase — such as four to eight words. There is a lot less competition for long-tail keywords, so you will rank higher, and should get even more relevant searches.

Once you have a solid list of keywords associated with your business, you can search for those terms associated with groups or find new community members by becoming more searchable yourself!

Search Engines	Don't overthink it – type your keywords or your keywords + the word "group" or "discussion" into search engines. You might be connected to groups on social media, educational resources, groups that meet in person (but have an online presence of some kind), etc.
Facebook	Enter your keyword in the search bar at the top of your Facebook page to begin. Top results (as determined by Facebook) will automatically appear, but you can refine your results by specifying person, location, or time to the left of your search results. Across the top, you can specify even further by selecting additional criteria like pages, events, videos, and even groups.
Twitter	Lists are the Twitter version of groups and they can be an effective way to make connections and keep yourself organized. From an individual profile, you can click on their lists and see what lists they have made public. You can subscribe to lists that interest you as well as identify individual followers you'd like to connect with. You can also create a list in Twitter, make it public and draw people to you by providing an informative and appealing list name. Twitter chats, explored in greater detail in *Marketing & Communications: The Right Social Media Content at the Right Time*, are another example of a group on Twitter – the major difference being that a Twitter chat is live! Like lists, you can find people with shared interests and valuable insights to connect with – and they can find you, too!

Instagram	Instagram isn't designed to support groups, but there is a search feature that might help you find people with similar interests. From there you can search hashtags and comment on posts. Begin by typing a keyword into the search field and then choose top people, tags, or places associated with the keyword. You'll be able to see activity associated with your keyword from multiple angles.
Pinterest	While there aren't groups on Pinterest, boards fulfill a similar purpose. You can create boards that will bring interested people to you or find pinners through existing boards. Connections and conversations are more difficult, but there are messaging options and you might end up connecting to a different, more conversation-friendly platform.
LinkedIn	The search bar on LinkedIn allows you to narrow your results when searching key terms and "groups" is one of your choices. You might eventually search for your keywords associated with posts or companies, but a great place to start is by searching for your keyword in a group.
Other:	Are there sites related to your industry that support collaboration? Is there a popular social media platform we didn't discuss here that is a great fit for your audience? Add it to your list!

Groups are typically easy to join and leave if they aren't a great fit. The more time you commit to the group and the more active a member you are, the more benefits you will receive. However, just like the members of the community you are trying to build, you only have so much time, so you have to spend it wisely. Carefully monitor your ROI and stick with the groups that yield positive results for you.

Get Referrals

Once you have even a small community started, you have the opportunity to build membership from within. It's likely that your current community members have at least one friend or coworker who has similar interests and would like to join your community. Will your current community members think to invite them to the group? They might. But you can increase the chances that they will reach out by suggesting they invite friends to the community, tag friends interested in specific conversations, or share posts. Never underestimate the power of directly asking for help from the people who support you.

Chapter 3 Discussion

1. Consider each of the four RTM categories – planned, watchlist, everyday, and opportunistic. Identify at least one possible event related to your community for each category.

2. Which groups could help you find new community members? List at least three that you are already active in and three new groups you'd like to explore.

3. How could you motivate your current members to refer people to your community? Are there benefits to being part of your community that you could emphasize to increase referrals?

Chapter 4

Engage Your Existing Followers

Evangelists and Loafers

Once you find members, remember that you have to work to keep them. We'll talk about this again related to creating meaningful content, but acknowledging contributions can go a long way to maintaining an engaged community. It's similar to the basic marketing principle, "It's more expensive to find new customers than to keep existing ones." Once you have community members, keep them – or you'll have to work twice as hard to replace them!

Within your audience and even your community, you will identify members who are either evangelists or loafers. They are on opposite ends of the activity spectrum – loafers being inactive, passive members and evangelists being constant contributors. People fall in different places on the spectrum and may move up and down the spectrum as conditions in their own lives change. But all community members are valuable and with careful planning, all of their contributions can be helpful.

Evangelists - highly active

People fall in different places on the spectrum and even move up and down the spectrum as conditions in their own lives change.

Loafers - low engagement

If you have identified a loafer – someone who has always been or recently became inactive – but you believe that they have something unique and valuable to share with the community, consider engaging their expertise directly. For example, if you have a statistician in your group who you know is active in at least one other group but hasn't contributed to your conversations in a while, try posting their article and tagging them. You might ask for their opinion on a specific topic or connect them with another group member if you think the introduction could be mutually beneficial.

You might think evangelists are the easy group to manage. After all, they're so happy, they can't stop talking about you, so they probably don't need much attention, right? That isn't true at all – in fact, that's a dangerous myth to fall for. Evangelists are a valuable resource, but if they are ignored, you risk them taking their commitment to an organization more likely to appreciate their contribution. Simple things like responding to their messages, sharing their contributions, and publicly acknowledging their commitment will help them feel appreciated. It also shows others how well you treat your community members and makes becoming an active member of your groups that much more appealing.

Stay Active

While seeking out community members through the techniques outlined in the previous chapter, it's important to simply stay active in the communities you have. If you choose to be present on a platform, check in daily or multiple times a day if it is a particularly active time in your business. Maintain personal communications by connecting directly with people on the platforms and keep the community as a whole interested by sharing meaningful content.

A few simple ways to stay active include:

- **Connecting members who might benefit from knowing each other.** For example, in your community, you might have two members who have a common interest but don't know each other yet. Tagging them both in a post or comment as an introduction is a great way to support individual community members and to show everyone the value of being an active community member.

- **Ask and answer questions.** You can pose fun questions like creative uses for your product or informative questions related to challenges in your industry as long as they are interesting enough to your readers that they will respond.

- **Share posts from your community members.** There are so many alert systems available, you may not even have to go looking for their blog posts, videos, or success stories!

    o You may receive alerts automatically if your community member tags you – respond, share, and contribute to that community member's post. If they thought of your group, the topic is probably a great fit for your community.

    o On many platforms, you can also click right through to a community member's profile – an easy way to see what your active community members are doing. For example, when reviewing your Twitter analytics, you might click through to your Top Follower's account. From there, you could easily see if they've recently tweeted a video, graphic, or blog post they created.

    o You can also use systems like Google Alerts that will let you know when individual names or organizations you've chosen appear online. For example, if you entered General Mills as an organization you'd like to be alerted about, you'd receive an alert each time they were in the news. Some of this content would be perfect for sharing and some of it wouldn't, but you'd have a nicely organized list to choose from.

    o Instead of an alert system, you might prefer to pull your own data – and there are tools for that, too!

Sites like Social Mention aggregate content from across the web and allow you to enter search terms. If you'd rather choose when you gather your content, for example, you might reserve Tuesday afternoon to search for the latest news on General Mills.

However you access your community members' great accomplishments, be sure to promote them within your group. It will make them feel appreciated and it will demonstrate to others that you're genuinely interested in the accomplishments of the group.

- **Invite community members to post – and support them when they do!** There's nothing worse than putting up a post that doesn't get any engagement. If you invite your community members to contribute, be sure to respond – and encourage others on your team to respond – to what they share. This will encourage future sharing from them and others in the group.

Leveraging Contests

Social media campaigns are discussed in greater detail in the NISM books *Project Management: How can you establish and maintain organized social media projects and campaigns?* and *Marketing & Communications: The Right Social Media Content at the Right Time,* but there are a few things you can do within your campaigns to strengthen and build your online communities.

1. Choose a prize that's meaningful to your community as opposed to appealing to the general public – something like branded swag or an early release of an upcoming book. While some contests target increasing your reach and just gaining exposure, a contest with a prize that's meaningful to your community is more likely to generate conversation and excitement.

2. Associate your contest with a custom hashtag that will further bring the group together. You might even continue the hashtag after the contest if you want to keep a good conversation going!

3. In the planning stage of your contest, set a SMART goal related to your community. This will help you remember to consider community development throughout your planning and analysis process. (Need a refresher on SMART goals? Check out the NISM book *Strategic Planning: How can SMART goals, an STP Analysis, and KPIs help you create the perfect social media plan?*)

4. Make entering easy and make it easy to share! Remember that your community members probably know people with similar interests. If you can create a contest that's easy to share, they're more likely to get their friends involved – and those friends may become valuable community members!

Any variety of value-added activities will increase the chances that you'll build your community by growing your audience. That same activity will help you keep your active members as well!

Chapter 4 Discussion

1. Consider your current community or a community that you're actively engaged in as a member. What content or conversations do you engage in? What motivates you to participate?

2. Have you ever left a community you were once an active member of? If so, why did you leave? Is there anything that could have been done to get you to stay? What did you learn that could be applied to the communities you manage?

Part Two

Growth through Engagement

Chapter 5

What Causes Community Members to Engage?

P eople need a reason to stay engaged in a community. Individual reasons will vary – even within the community – but the reason has to exist and they have to be aware of it on some level. At minimum, their participation in your community costs them time. Through their support, they might also be sharing their reputation. In return, the community must benefit them.

What value might people find in a community?

The perceived value members find in any community will be the source of their motivation and the extent of their motivation is what will determine whether or not they are active in your community. Every community member – whether they realize it or not – is balancing the personal and professional commitments against how they will benefit from being a member of the community. This may not be the only factor that determines the extent to which they contribute, but it is the starting place.

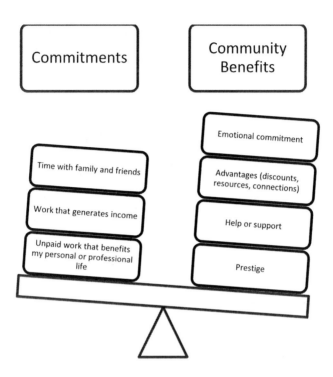

Advantages

Being part of a community often provides the member with some kind of advantage: for example, early access to information, monetary discounts, or industry updates from leading experts. A perceived advantage could come in any format as long as the community member views it as valuable.

Help or Support

Some communities revolve around a challenge, product, or topic that generates a lot of questions. These communities have the opportunity to become wildly strong because if the community manager or another member *solves* a problem, the community's value increases. Similarly, if a community member *contributes a solution*, the community becomes a place where a person can feel useful and appreciated. Within this community design, members can be both recipients and providers and that naturally fosters and exceptionally strong group.

Emotional Commitment

If your community members are part of your group because of their commitment to a cause or connection to an industry, their motivation is tied to feeling like they're contributing to the success of something that's important to them. If their family lost their home due to a house fire, the fear and pain they experienced will stay with them forever and will likely motivate them to help others avoid a similar tragedy. If the community is made up of members of one profession – people passionate about the work they do – they likely spend their days focused on professional success. They will appreciate your similar level of commitment to advancing the field and will support your work. Whatever the cause, the most important factor that will motivate community members is the feeling that you're supporting the cause that is so important to them.

Prestige or Credibility

When I became a small business owner, I realized for the first time just how important my reputation was! After spending a decade working in an organization, I had forgotten how often people connected with me, listened to what I had to say, and asked for my advice based on my reputation. Starting fresh, I realized my new audience didn't know anything about me – and had no reason to trust me. Becoming an active part of communities was one way I chose to establish my credibility – and you might find members in your community with similar goals. The best part about community members interested in establishing themselves is that they are typically fantastic contributors! Once you establish a rapport with them, you can reach out with specific questions, connect them to other community members, or just sit back and allow them to contribute content. If you provide enough direction and support, this kind of community design can truly be win-win.

Enjoyment

Your community may be filled with very active members who simply enjoy the product or industry your business operates in. If you make an amazing hiking boot or the best baking pans in the business, you have an opportunity to harness the excitement your community already has for your industry. These are also communities that often have creative ideas that will strengthen your brand.

What motivates your community?

Are you having trouble fitting your community into just one category of motivation? You're not alone. There are many communities that provide help and an emotional connection. People often enjoy the industry they work in and genuinely have fun while establishing their own credibility. It's less important that you choose one than to know the different language and content that will keep members of your community engaged.

Motivation	Language	Content	Challenges
☐ Advantages ☐ Help/Support ☒ Emotional Commitment ☐ Prestige/ Credibility ☐ Enjoyment	you helped us results thank you change	Stories (with pictures) of real people the community helped and details of how they were helped	Stories are very similar; how can we make each one unique?

After reading the previous descriptions of the potential motivating factors that influence your community members, identify one or two motivation categories, keywords you could use to connect with that community member, and at least one idea for content that would be of interest to them. Also note any challenges associated with the technique.

Motivation	Keywords	Content	Challenges
☐ Advantages ☐ Help/Support ☐ Emotional 　Commitment ☐ Prestige/ 　Credibility ☐ Enjoyment			
☐ Advantages ☐ Help/Support ☐ Emotional 　Commitment ☐ Prestige/ 　Credibility ☐ Enjoyment			

What other factors influence their participation?

It's important, too, to recognize external factors that influence a community member's ability and willingness to engage. For example, a community member may be active for a year and then suddenly disappear. Have they suddenly become disenchanted with your community? Did you do something to upset them? Do they believe the competitor has more to offer?

Any of these things could be true, but it's also possible that they had a baby, got a new job, or started volunteering in their hometown so they have less free time than before. To keep as many of your community members as possible engaged, keep your ROI high by remembering the following tips:

- **Make whatever motivates them to remain active (support, prestige, etc.) easy to get.** The more difficult it is to engage in a community, the less likely community members will remain. It's possible – even likely – that this will change, so be sure to continue to listen to your community for new ideas.
- **Identify multiple connection points.** If your community primarily engages on one platform, have at least one

other way of communicating as well. For example, if you have a heavy presence on Twitter, occasionally run a campaign to collect email addresses. Send emails to the list quarterly to approach the community in a different way and to re-engage anyone who may not be on Twitter as much as they used to be.

- **Routinely collect feedback.** As the community manager, there might be things you can do to better support members. The easiest way to identify those opportunities is by asking. A simple model like Start, Stop, Continue (asking members to identify one thing the community should start doing, one thing they should stop doing, and one thing they should continue doing) allows people to quickly send simple suggestions that can easily lead to an improved community.

Why do people commit and then not deliver?

In 2016, I began informally investigating why so many people commit to communities and then choose not to fulfill their promise. I was hearing stories of disappointment from non-profits, community groups, and even business owners. They shared stories of people who had initially been highly engaged on social media platforms, expressed an interest in sharing content from the community, or planned on supporting other members or becoming content contributors only to underdeliver, disengage, or disappear completely before the support was given. Many community managers were left baffled by the change of heart.

I conducted online surveys (separate questions for employees and leaders) and in-person interviews and uncovered several themes associated with community members whose expressed commitment never translated to action.

They didn't fully understand the commitment.

Whether the leader didn't explain the commitment well, the actual commitment was unclear initially, or the community member wasn't listening, many community members admitted that – once they started engaging – it was more than they could realistically commit to. For example, a friend of mine began participating in an online weight loss community and initially enjoyed the motivation and inspiration she received through the group. But over time, the frequency of the posts (daily) and participation required (weekly check-ins) took more time than she was willing to commit. I heard examples of needing more time than originally estimated, not having the knowledge (or willingness to gain the knowledge) to complete the work, and discovering that the more work they did, the more work they generated for themselves. The commitment simply became unmanageable.

The personal cost and/or risk was too great.

This sounds very dramatic – but it's actually a very common challenge professionals face. For example, a small business owner may like the idea of actively participating in your community because of what he can learn. After a few weeks, he might see clients or competitors in the community and worry that his questions or contributions could somehow put his professional reputation at risk (by making him appear to be biased or uninformed, for example). As with educational environments, for people to fully participate in a community, they have to feel safe. You might find active community members transition to a passive audience state simply because they feel their professional reputation is at stake.

An external factor derailed their progress.

You might engage a community member at the perfect time in their personal and professional life. They may be genuinely interested, active, and engaged – until one day they aren't. It is possible they lost interest in your community or are now more fully engaged with your competitor. It is more likely something happened in their personal or professional life that either changed their routine or limited the amount of time they could commit to your community.

> But an audience member may not transition to an active community member if you can't engage them on multiple occasions in a short period of time.

They never developed a routine.

We are all creatures of habit. Even those of us who have a different schedule every day rely on consistency and pattern to some degree. Our community participation is no different. Personally, I check in with communities when I'm waiting in lines (grocery store, car wash, etc.) and in the evenings when I'm too tired to write or grade papers! I developed these patterns without even thinking about it and your community members will, too. But an audience member may not transition to an active community member if you can't engage them on multiple occasions in a short period of time. For example, if you're managing a Facebook group, you might post a teaser a week before you share big news, followed by an article related to the big news, and then start a countdown to your big reveal. Whether they catch one or all of the posts, the multiple tries increase your chances of a meaningful connection.

The excitement for the idea faded.

This is the challenge I see most often. A community member bursts onto the scene with an unparalleled interest and commitment. You're thrilled to have an advocate of this caliber in the group. And then, as dramatically as they appeared, they disappear. I always encourage community managers to reflect on specific content or conversations that could have caused someone to separate from the group, but it's important to recognize that sometimes the community member simply fell in love with the idea of the group but was never going to be an active member. After seeing this a few times, I started to notice people who engaged passionately for short periods of time with group after group. It seemed to be in their personality to burn brightly while things are still new and exciting.

Whatever causes your community members to come and go, it's important to learn from them and then move on. It is unlikely that your community will ever be the most important thing in a person's personal or professional life, so it's natural for their engagement to change over time. Fortunately, there are always new people ready to bring their energy to your group. And, if you keep listening to your community and implementing their ideas to make the group meaningful, your ability to stay current with the industry is your best shot at re-engaging anyone who has become less active!

Chapter 5 Discussion

1. Review the list of reasons why people participate in communities at the beginning of this chapter. Which reasons are most applicable to your community members? Are there other reasons not listed that motivate your community?

2. Ask your community the Start, Stop, Continue question. What did you learn?

3. What are three things you can do in your community to help mitigate the effect of contributors leaving the community?

Chapter 6

Community Content

O nce you determine why your community members arrive at and stay with your group, it's important to focus on the content that will best support them. In 2012, NISM published their first textbook and highlighted several key considerations for creating community content:

- Maintain a consistent voice
- Focus on developing fans, not just followers
- Be genuine – show interest in your community and its members
- Tell stories

If you'd like to read the details, we've included a small section of the original NISM book in the additional resources section at the end of this text. Many of the ideas are still applicable today! But the following is a list of specific suggestions we've seen help both small and large businesses gain traction in recent history. Depending on your industry and business, the different ideas may be of more or less interest to you, so we encourage you to consider what you know about your audience before choosing content types. That is the art and science of social media strategy – we can share what has worked for others and you can decide if it will work for you.

A great place to start is a quick industry audit. Research the following questions:

- What kinds of materials are your competitors sharing (informative blogs, videos, graphics, etc.)?

- Of the materials your competitors are sharing, what seems to get the most positive engagement?
- What kinds of materials are complementary businesses offering? For example, if you're a fitness studio, what kinds of offerings do popular exercise clothing and protein drinks share?
- What needs do your audience members express and how can you solve them?

A structured look like the above list can help you stay organized and identify what types of content your audience responds to and appreciates. Since so many things can be delivered via multiple mediums, this could be a great opportunity to make a small change that better serves your community. For example, you may realize very few people watch your videos past the first minute and yet you have a high download rate of checklists with the same content. You might choose to make shorter videos or invest your marketing dollars in creating a more intricate checklist. Whatever you decide, you will have done so based on your audience preferences.

Frequently Engage with Your Audience

The suggestions below have one thing in common: a reliance on frequency. It doesn't matter how good the content is if it is presented too infrequently. It won't help you build community if the opportunities to engage are too few. As you review the following suggestions, consider both what your audience will respond to as well as what you can realistically manage.

Create content that can be easily shared.
Each platform has unique sharing opportunities, so determining the best way to make your content "sharable" will be largely dependent on where you're hosting your information. On Facebook, there's a share button. On your website, you might need a plug-in. Twitter allows followers to retweet. The technical process varies, but the strategic approach is the

same. Communities need to provide content that can be easily shared from the platform the community member is using.

There are many obstacles that could potentially make sharing at worst impossible and at best annoying. If you have an approval process, are you sure it's necessary? Is your platform easy to use – and if it isn't, can you improve it? If possible, have an external individual attempt to share content and ask them for feedback about the process.

Suggest why people might want to share your content.

When you create content, you likely have several groups of people in mind who would benefit from what you created. If it's an infographic, blog post, video, or image, it serves a purpose, and you can't always trust that your readers will understand that purpose. For example, you might create a video about organizing your home office and post it in your remote work community. Other than remote workers, who else has a home office? In your video notes or post intro, suggest the viewer share the content with anyone they know who has a home office – business owners, sales professionals, and any other *specific* job titles that might trigger a connection for your reader. Your community members have people in their lives they care about and would happily share content that would be beneficial to others. Sometimes they just need specific direction to get them started.

Just ask.

Schedule surveys or polling – formal or informal, but always short – into your regular content generation. Ask your community what they'd like information about and give them a list of choices or an open text field. Ask if a specific article or topic is of interest to them and pay attention to the response (or lack of response).

Be interestED, not just interesting.

If you want your community members to care about you, try caring about them. You can't fake it: you have to do the work. Find causes, resources, and stories that are a gift to your community – not just content that helps you or your message. Make resources that will help your community – your gifts to them – 80% of your content and limit your asks to 20%. Marketers too often fall into the trap of talking about themselves and what their organization has to offer. It's easy content and it makes sense, right? While people are interested in hearing about you to some extent, it's more meaningful if you can focus on them and how you can make their lives better. A small change can make a huge difference.

> Make resources that will help your community – your gifts to them – 80% of your content and limit your asks to 20%.

Your original post could be:

> **Company Focused:** We're hosting a BOGO event in the month of June – stock up now before we run out!

> **Community Focused:** June is a big month for your client gifts, so we want to give you a break. Any purchase in June is eligible for a BOGO, so you can easily choose and ship high-quality gifts on any budget!

Your response to a community member's post could be:
"I'm ready for the conference – I even booked an extra night so I can stay and do some sightseeing after the event!"

> **Company Focused:** Be sure to post this on all your platforms and invite your friends! We want this to be the biggest year yet. See you soon!

> **Community Focused:** Awesome – did you get the list of conference perks? There are some local event deals listed that would be perfect for your extra day.

Make it easy and safe for community members to contribute.
Why do so many community managers believe they have to generate all of the content? Not only is that more work than inviting member contributions, it's also the opposite of being interested in what they have to say! Even if a community manager embraces the idea of inviting members to post, they may struggle getting started. Here are some tips for encouraging contributions.

1. **Give them ideas.** Try sharing a post that says, "Is anyone interested in (writing about, finding a video on, etc.) this topic?" For a lot of people, it's much easier to respond to a question than to choose a topic out of the blue. And it doesn't require quite as much courage because they already know you're interested in what they'll share!
2. **Praise people who do contribute.** If you have a community member who contributes, support them! Read or view their contribution and provide meaningful feedback, and then thank them for their thoughts. The acknowledgement will go a long way in getting them to contribute again and it will also let others know that you appreciate member contributions.

Promote Accomplishments.
Congratulate your community members on their accomplishments, ask for their specific expert opinions and shine a light on any work they're doing. A genuine show of support can boost your relationship with the community member and demonstrate to the wider audience that you care about the group members. If your community feels too large to keep track of details like this, consider setting up an alert system. Whether you receive messages when specific words, businesses, or people are mentioned, there are a number of tools that will deliver potential content right to your inbox.

You can also promote the accomplishments of people or organizations who aren't yet in your community but are doing work your members would be interested in. That mention might even lead to the individuals you were promoting to join your group!

Talk about other people, places, things, and ideas.
Do you remember the definition of a noun from your earliest English classes? The same definition – person, place, thing, or idea – can be a checklist for reaching outside your community to integrate valuable content. Conversations about others – their successes, tips and even challenges – can make your community discussions both interesting and informative. Sometimes people worry that talking about other people, groups, or ideas will lead to members leaving a community. In fact, the opposite is more likely. Your diversity of content and dedication to keeping everyone informed is more likely to make people trust you as their primary resource.

Presentation Sharing
Sharing presentations is an effective way to brainstorm ideas, create effective demonstrations, and work in real-time with team members. While most people think of these as tools for completing class projects in a university classroom or presentations by a work team, they can also be a fantastic tool for educating and engaging your community.

Google Slides
Google Slides is a free presentation app available to anyone who has a Google account. Google Slides can be shared via a link or by adding others directly to the presentation. People can be assigned different editing permissions, which makes collaboration easy and low risk.

LinkedIn SlideShare
LinkedIn SlideShare describes itself as "a global hub of professional content." According to its website, it's "one of the top 100 most-visited websites in the world, with over 70

million unique visitors a month and 18 million uploads to date." The site further explains that SlideShare works as a great marketing tool because it will "automatically optimize your content to get traction via search," but users are encouraged to promote their presentations through their own social channels.

Prezi

Prezi is a presentation software that focuses on using "big picture" designs to reinforce the message of the presentation. Prezis can be private or public – making them great for internal team work or for easily sharing an important message from your community.

Our Interview with Prezi

We wanted to gain additional insight from an expert in the field of presentation sharing, so we reached out to Brett Smith, Prezi's Global PR and Communications Manager. We asked him about the functions Prezi has to offer and how people successfully use the tool to build community. Here's what he had to say:

Please describe any/all collaborative functions Prezi currently has to offer.

In Prezi Business, co-editing and commenting features support real-time collaboration and eliminate the need for version control, allowing users to talk to each other directly in their Prezis, no matter their location. Prezi Business also stores presentations in the cloud, letting users sort, select, or link them together from a single location. This content can then be shared with colleagues for collaborative development, and with customers who may then bring it into their own organizations to continue the conversation as needed.

Why is the collaborative element so important to Prezi?

The business (and education) landscape is packed with tools that give teams tons of data, but in the midst of all the slides, we too often forget about the need to engage our audience with a collaborative experience—not a canned speech. Great businesses are powered by meaningful conversations, and moving beyond the strict presenter/audience model will help ideas flourish. Prezi enables meaningful, two-way communications by showing how ideas and data connect to each other in a dynamic map-like structure, inviting the audience to choose the direction of the conversation and the presenter to do the steering. With Prezi, you can determine and focus on the content that matters most to each audience every time you present, making it easier to cut through the noise and make an impact with your message.

When you consider feedback from Prezi users or even your own experiences, what are the greatest challenges people face when using collaborative presentation software? And for each of the challenges, have you seen successful solutions?

Presentations are an essential part of business communications, and there's plenty of evidence that suggests changing up the old office stack's way of presenting (one-way dialogue using slides and bullet points) can have a huge impact on overall success. According to the RAIN Group, for example, sales professionals can increase sales by collaborating with prospects instead of talking at them, and ION Interactive recently found that twice as many consumers say that interactive content is more memorable than static. Collaboration is key for Prezi's customers—and our Prezis have been shared the world over.

The opportunities for building community through presentation-sharing platforms are tremendous, and platforms like Prezi are working hard to educate everyone about best practices.

Providing meaningful information and an opportunity to easily collaborate can be a great tool for any community, and here are a few examples of what communities might do:

- Create an educational presentation or series of presentations and share them with your community. Branding the content will help you get your name out and sharing your hard work will help strengthen your position in your community.
- Encourage community members to share their presentations within the group. Many communities strive for a common goal across the globe. If someone in Minnesota creates a presentation about supporting local businesses, a person in Florida would probably benefit from some or all of the content. They may even have some suggestions for the original presentation!
- Invite community members to create a presentation together. I was part of a group once that created a Prezi introducing a new concept. We all had access to the presentation and specific elements we were responsible for contributing. One person did manage the overall design to ensure consistency, but the workload was otherwise balanced evenly amongst us. It was an interesting presentation created with very little work for any one person.

What is good content?

It seems like the solution to every social media challenge is to create good content. Do you want a more active community? Do you want more followers? Trying to increase engagement? Interested in having people read your messages? All you have to do is create good content!

As you can see by the motivating factors and content ideas outlined in this book, there is no one right answer that works for everyone. Good content – content that is received well by your community and leads to engagement – will be different in look, feel, and format depending on what your specific audience prefers. There are some themes – engaging often, providing value, providing recognition, etc. – but those themes look different in every industry. As a social media professional, your role requires that you consider these concepts and adjust them based on what you know about your community to maximize success.

A Bold Community We Can Learn From

Did you know that Star Trek fans are often credited with creating the first media fandom? Viewers were interested in networking with others who enjoyed the show, so the show's creator helped them make that happen.

When the show was cancelled after three seasons, fans created and shared their own stories through art, music, newsletters, and zines. In 1972, Joan Winston helped organize the first Star Trek convention – expecting a few hundred people to attend – only to end up with 3,000 fans (some of whom were, of course, in costume).

Is your community on the brink of forming a Trekkie convention? Probably not. But you can still learn from the Star Trek community. They encouraged their fans to express their commitment in ways that worked for them and – by not restricting their approach – enjoyed the benefits of their creativity.

I knew a volunteer community manager who excitedly took on the challenge of helping a nonprofit group create an online presence. She was thrilled to be able to start from scratch – the group had no online activity. And even better, the board and small membership of about 100 people were so excited to see what she could do.

Over the course of a year, she implemented campaigns, programs, and various techniques to boost engagement within the community and every effort failed. When she considered what could possibly cause an active community whose members expressed high levels of commitment and excitement to not participate, she decided it must be a lack of understanding. Social media was new to them, so she began providing detailed instructions for how they could participate and why that participation would help the group.

Again, all her efforts failed.

Eventually she identified the real problem by carefully researching similar groups and analyzing their behavior. What she realized was that the group was made up of people who did genuinely want the nonprofit to succeed, but they were more committed to their individual success (which was an understandable choice). The community manager learned that the community members perceived the personal risk to be too great. When she asked them to share an upcoming event, they ignored her request because – though they wanted to help – they thought sharing the event would mean pestering their friends. When she encouraged them to spread the word about a publication from one of the group members, they pretended not to get her messages because – again, though they wanted to help – sharing another person's success didn't directly benefit them and, in fact, it may even make their own accomplishments seem less valuable.

Though no one told her directly, these feelings soon became obvious. She noticed that participation was highest when members had an opportunity to give advice or recommend the work of someone they knew personally. Their personal reputation was too important to risk – and yet the community manager knew their association with the group would only boost their credibility. Here's how she altered her messaging so that she could deliver what her community would identify as good content:

> **Events:** Each event focused first on the professional credentials and experience of the speaker instead of the content they'd be presenting. That was shared, too, but it was secondary. The community manager realized

that, for this community, a person's reputation was more important than the topic they were presenting.

Articles, Publications, and Various Works of Other Community Members: The community manager realized she had to help people see that they could experience "success by association" by engaging with posts from other community members. When she shared this type of information, she emphasized the credibility of the publishing source and how the community as a whole benefited from being associated with the accomplishment. For many, this brought about the realization that their peers' success was something they could safely share without risking their own reputation.

General Content: Using what she observed, she also set up a routine posting of questions to be discussed within the group. By this time, she had learned enough about the group to identify what challenges they were likely experiencing – whether they would admit it or not – so she could share content that was perceived as an advantage associated with the group. Community members could share tips and boost their reputation and others could learn from their responses without having to admit they needed the help. Both helped community members develop the habit of checking in with the group regularly.

In this instance, content only became successful when the community manager finally understood the priorities and concerns of the community members and adjusted accordingly.

Community Managers...take care of yourselves!

One final thought on the importance of creating valuable content for your community. As a community manager, you're the heart of the activity – creating, directing, and inspiring contributions. To continue to successfully generate that kind of energy, you have to take care of yourself. You must manage your schedule carefully and make sure you unplug when you're tired or overwhelmed. You need to put systems in place to ensure that you evaluate your efforts and continue to improve without being too hard on yourself. You have to routinely do things that inspire you, or your ability to inspire will run out.

In the example above, the community manager was trying to solve problems that didn't exist. She was supporting a community in ways that made sense to her, and yet the community members had no interest in engaging. By the time she eventually identified what the community was really interested in – and what she could do to support their needs – she had been disappointed so many times, it didn't matter to her.

Because the leadership was busy with other commitments and actually had a lot of faith in her ability to figure everything out, the community manager eventually burned out. She was disappointed by all of her failed attempts. She felt she took too long to arrive at a solution. The win she eventually got just wasn't enough to offset all the disappointments.

The last time I was on a plane, I listened to a flight attendant deliver the standard pre-flight safety announcements. My thoughts wandered back to my conversations with that community manager and I realized the second valuable lesson she taught me.

"...if you are travelling with someone who requires assistance, secure your mask on first, and then assist the other person. Keep your mask on until a uniformed crew member advises you to remove it."

If your role is to support and care for others, you have to remember to care for yourself first. Why is the advice to ensure your own safety first – ignored by most – so important? Because, of course, if you lose consciousness or become disoriented, you won't be able to help anyone *and* you'll poten-tially create more work for the rescue team. And yet our nat-ural reflex is often to first care for the people we believe need us. In actuality, they need us to stay healthy and alert more than anything else.

The same applies to community management. If you feel solely responsible for supporting a community, you might stop caring for yourself. You may not read as much because you're so focused on writing. You may skip attending a con-tinuing education class because you feel pressured to create resources. You might slip into the habit of one-way conversa-tions because you're so focused on being a source of informa-tion you forget to take the time to listen.

What could she have done differently? It's hard to say what would have worked, but she could have tried asking the other volunteers in the group for support and feedback. She could have sought out a mentor or asked marketing profession-als outside of the group – her trusted peers – for their ideas. She felt the online community was her responsibility and yet, because she didn't seek out support, she's now unable to help others.

Make time to collaborate with your team. Talk about what's working and what's not working. Have each team member bring one new and creative idea they read about to the meet-ing. And if you don't have an internal team to rely on, find a community of marketing professionals outside of your organi-zation to collaborate with. Don't look for a support group or business owners who will just tell you you're doing a great job. Find a group of people or a mentor who understands your busi-ness and can provide you with concrete and practical feedback.

If you make time for your own professional development – your oxygen mask – you'll be better equipped to support your community. And if you don't, it won't be long before you're unable to provide support to anyone.

Chapter 6 Discussion

1. What content does your community appreciate and engage with? List at least one type of content you're currently using successfully and one type you plan to use in the future because you believe your community will value it.

2. What can you do in your role as a community manager to avoid burnout?

Part Three

Give More Than You Receive

Chapter 7

People Will Remember What You Do

"I've learned that people will forget what you said, people will forget what you did, but people will never forget how you made them feel."

– Maya Angelou

R elationships are critical in any role a social media professional has. Remember the scale we looked at in Chapter 5? As people weigh their personal and professional commitment against the benefits of being an active part of your community, the relationship you've established with them will be a substantial influencing factor. Do they feel important? Are their contributions appreciated? Do they benefit from knowing you and others in the community?

Responding to contributions

As a community manager, you have an opportunity to strengthen your group by responding to what others share. Initially, this will be challenging because it will take time to foster an environment of contributors. Eventually, it will be challenging because your community members will share so much, it will be hard to keep up! Here are a few techniques you can use to make sure you remember to continually give back to your community.

Read and Respond – Internal

When your community members share content, respond in a meaningful way. Avoid simply liking what they share if possible. Read or watch the contribution and respond in a way that demonstrates that you took the time to look at what they shared.

Read and Respond – External

Make the effort to engage with your community members outside of your platform. When you're researching content, you're bound to cross paths with community members. You might even go to community member organizations or other groups for content. While you're there, engage with their posts.

Whether you're responding to an internal or external post, take the time to contribute thoughtfully. You don't have to change the world in 140 characters or scrutinize every contribution you make, but whenever possible, contribute to the conversation – don't just add to the noise on social media.

- Agree and share specifically what resonated with you. Perhaps you have an example from your own life that would further the conversation?
- Disagree and say why! You don't have to agree with everything your peers say. Two people may be tremendously impressed with each other and agree on very little if they recognize that their ability to disagree respectfully and intelligently is how they'll both stay at the top of their game.
- Ask a question. If you engaged with a post and it made you think of new questions, that's an amazing compliment. Share your thoughts – they might have an answer for you or you might help them further their work.

Chapter 7 Discussion

1. Review recent communications within a community you are either managing or an active member of. When did the community manager or other members of the community provide feedback that would have made someone feel recognized and appreciated?

2. In the same review, look for missed opportunities. Where do you see contributions or conversations that could have been better supported by the community manager?

Chapter 8

Engagement Tools

There are opportunities within your day-to-day social media activity to promote engagement within your community. A longer list of content and engagement ideas for various social media platforms is available in the NISM book *Marketing & Communications: The Right Social Media Content at the Right Time*, but the following are platform-specific tips specifically aimed at giving back to your community and increasing engagement.

Staying Organized

One tool specific tool in *Marketing & Communications: The Right Social Media Content at the Right Time* you might find particularly useful is a detailed process outlined for creating an editorial calendar to help you and your team stay organized. Essentially, an editorial calendar prevents you from ad hoc posting and ensures you maintain a consistent presence and flow of activity. A few elements of the editorial calendar reviewed here will also help you focus on contributing to your community on a regular basis in a meaningful way.

- **Add routine communication to your calendar.** If your group responds well to #TBT on Thursdays, make a note to engage in at least one conversation with the hashtag. If the weekend is typically very active in your community, check in on Friday to see what people need from the community to be successful.

- **Plan some of your engagement questions.** You still want to respond in-the-moment with conversational questions based on what your community is talking about, but you can write some thoughtful questions you know will start a conversation and have them ready for whenever you need them.
- **Highlight when your community is most active on which platforms.** The consistent content you organize through your editorial calendar will help you stay active on all your platforms, but you can also use your editorial calendar to focus on the platforms most likely to have conversations you should join. Once you've identified those platforms and focused your energy on real-time engagement, you'll also be able to identify key members of the community you should engage with.
- **Note any events related to your community you'll attend or engage with in real-time.** Include hashtags, key people to follow, links to the event information, and any other critical information that will help you engage fully in the event.
- **Link your calendar to additional resources.** Create a shared folder with images or a document with content that works well with the potential community engagement you've identified. For example, your community might respond well to motivational quotes, and a document with a list of researched quotes could be linked to Monday and the hashtag #MotivationMonday.

Sample Editorial Calendar Highlighting Community Engagement Opportunities

The following editorial calendar is for the community of customers who are advocates for Home Décor, a remodeling organization that focuses on restoring old homes. The calendar is an example of how community engagement can be organized to ensure meaningful and consistent messaging for the community by involving members and employees, and providing activities the community would be interested in.

*To emphasize the focus on community engagement, the regularly scheduled content is not visible. A sample of what this might look like as a complete editorial calendar can be found in the additional resources of this book.

	Monday	Tuesday	Wednes	Thursday	Friday	Saturday	Sunday
First week of the month – focus on starting strong							
			Connect with **Closet Con key people**		Closet-Con Conference **Website Hashtags and key people**		
Combat the mid-month slump with 1 inspirational member story each day	Tag story subject	Tag story subject	Tag story subject	Tag story subject	Tag story subject	Tag story subject	Tag story subject
				Follow International Home Redecoration chats			
Last week of the month – focus on planning for next month.							

Key

- The far left column is a place for reminders that apply to the entire week. Home Décor knows their community well enough to know that there are periods of time each month where people are more or less motivated to work on their homes, so conversations are geared toward boosting energy and interest at key times.
- Monday and Thursday are hotlinks. Monday is linked to a share folder with inspiring images for #MotivationMonday. Thursday is linked to a document filled with facts and images related to the organization's history.

- A big convention showcasing closet options is happening the third week of the month. The Wednesday before the event, the community manager will engage key people associated with the conference. The day of the event, the team will follow the conference hashtag and engage with key attendees. All of the information needed to engage is organized in a separate document linked to the editorial calendar.
- The fourth Thursday of the month is International Home Redecoration Day. The community manager isn't sure how popular that will be but is going to watch that day for possible chats or hashtags to follow.

There are many potential conversations a social media strategist and marketing team could engage in, and the rest of this chapter is devoted to practical tips and ideas for different platforms. But it's important for social media professionals to realize that keeping your conversations organized will keep you from missing opportunities and help your community better understand what they can expect from you.

Engagement Tactics

Your Website

Many businesses think of their website as a destination – the place you send your community members *to*, not necessarily the place where they engage. But why? Designed correctly, your website can be one of the best ways to engage your community. After all, it's the hub of your business and the place people are most likely to go to learn more about you. To maximize engagement on your website:

- **Give them something to do.** When they get to your website, will they immediately see something they want to click on – maybe a video or link? You can increase their interest in your community by quickly giving them something to do on your site. And the longer they hang out on your website, the more likely they are to become engaged with your message.
- **Make your site easy to navigate.** Especially if you have visitors who come to your site with a specific mission

in mind, make what they're looking for easy to find. The classic trick of putting the products everyone wants to buy in the back of the store (so you have to walk by all of the other products to get there) doesn't work online. The average consumer expects fast answers, and if your site can't deliver, they will move on.

- **Provide related content.** In some format (links, a blog roll, etc.) provide your visitors with access to related materials you think they'll find valuable. This is a great way to demonstrate that you're a committed member of your community interested in all conversations – not just the ones you've started.

- **Link to your social platforms.** This may seem obvious, but it's a good idea to take a fresh look at how visible your social media platforms are on your website. If you add or move content, you might lose the links in the shuffle. If your social media sites aren't easily identified, you'll miss the potential community members who want to connect with you on the platform of their choice.

- **Invite them to read *and comment* on your blog.** There aren't many websites that have a place for community members to contribute (unless the site itself is some kind of community board). However, you can host your blog on your website and invite people to add comments. And, yes, I mean *literally invite them to comment*. In each blog, when you share your posts on social media sites, and maybe even on your blog page, remind them how much you value their comments.

- **Capture email addresses.** It's a classic – but still valuable today. If someone is interested in you enough to visit your site, offer them the opportunity to regularly connect with you with minimal effort on their part. You might offer something like a white paper or tips sheet in exchange for their email, but what you're really doing is making it easier for them to receive updates in the future about the amazing work you're doing.

Newsletters and Email Campaigns

In a study conducted by The Radicati Group, Inc., researchers discovered that, "In 2015, the number of business emails sent and received per user per day totals 122 emails. This figure continues to show growth and is expected to average 126 messages sent and received per business user by the end of 2019." There are two ways to think about that data. You might think email is an active platform for professionals. You might also think that with that much competition, there's no way your message will stand out. To a certain extent, both are true. Here are some tips to make the most of your newsletter and email campaigns.

- **Provide something that's actually valuable.** If you want people to appreciate being part of your community, give them something they can actually use. You have to do more than write an article filled with good advice. If your market is teachers, give them a one-page document they could print and use in their classroom this afternoon. If your market is mechanics, send a logic tree that outlines how to answer customer questions that a shop manager could use in their next team meeting. Don't send content that requires them to do more work. Give them a gift. (And, by the way, brand any printable you send so that, even if the original recipient doesn't give you credit, the readers will see your information.)
- **Summarize industry highlights.** Do you ever feel like there is so much happening in the world, there's no way to keep up with everything? As a community manager, you have the opportunity to be the resource that compiles the most important information in a "top 10" list. If your community members are feeling overwhelmed,

they will come to rely on you to stay up-to-date in their industry.

- **Make it easy to share.** Once you've created these amazing pieces of content, make them easy to share. Using language ("Share this with anyone you know who...") and the tools within your email management system (e.g., share buttons for social media, "forward this to a friend" options) remind your community members that *they* might have community members who would enjoy this.

Surveys

A few of the NISM books talk about how surveys can be powerful tools for gathering useful information for your platforms, but they can be an incredible tool for community building as well. A survey is a way for you to let your community know their opinion matters. To emphasize community building with your surveys, follow these tips:

- **Tell them why you're asking.** So many businesses take their customers' time for granted; you have the opportunity to stand out by briefly explaining the value of your survey. Consider the difference between a survey explanation that says, "Your opinion about the dairy market is important," and one that says, "In the last 5 years we've seen a slow decline in specific dairy product purchases. Identifying the reason behind this trend is critical to the success of our industry and we believe you're the greatest resource we have for uncovering that information."
- **Tell them why *their* opinion matters.** Diffusion of responsibility is a concept you might hear about in many industries, but it's particularly applicable to social media. Simply stated, it refers to the tendency people have to avoid action because they believe someone else will respond. Telling potential survey respondents why

you want them *specifically* to chime in will encourage them to participate. And if they really are invested in your community and your mission, they'll want to help and they'll respect you more for contributing in a meaningful way to the organization's mission.

- **Keep your surveys short – and tell your audience just how short they are.** No matter how committed a person is, they only have so much time. If you ask someone to complete a survey or a 2-minute survey, you're more likely to get responses for the 2-minute survey.
- **Offer to share the results.** Always give back! Remember, to be a good community manager, your community has to understand that you give more than you take. If you're going to ask them to share their feedback, you should at least offer to share the results – even if they don't take you up on it. But if they do express an interest in the results, they will share their contact information, and that is one more way to keep them active and connected in your community.

Blogs

Many writers abandon their blog because they aren't able to attract enough readers. And even if they do have readers, it can be frustrating to write post after post without receiving any feedback. Blogging can be an amazing way to support and grow your community, though. It's an easy-to-manage platform that allows you to share significant chunks of material with your audience.

- **Mix up your delivery method.** You don't have to *write* your blog post every week. Record a vlog, or post a graphic. Sometimes just changing your format is what your audience needs.
- **Make sharing easy *throughout* your post.** Aside from suggesting people share your post, you can make it easy for them to share parts of your posts. Sites like

clicktotweet allow you to highlight key phrases, images, or stats and, with a few clicks, readers can share the sentiment with their followers. There are multiple options available, but the idea is to make your blog post and individual parts of your blog post interesting and easy to pass on to others!

- **Guest blog.** One way to expand your community is to write – directly or indirectly – about your community on someone else's blog. If your organization offers a product that can solve a problem, find a group that's interested in the solution you offer. Do you sell green household cleaners? You could easily find groups focused on environmental issues that would love to hear from you. At minimum, you can share your community information and you might increase your audience. At best, you might find people interested in becoming active members.
- **Invite someone to guest blog for you.** It's a little harder to find guest bloggers than it is to guest blog, but if you put a call out on your social media channels and emphasize what's in it for them (exposure to a new group, boosted credibility, a great addition for their LinkedIn profile, etc.), you might find someone willing to contribute a post to your blog. That, of course, expands your reach, but it also reminds people of your commitment to sharing information from multiple sources to best serve the community.
- **Read blogs, follow successful bloggers, and learn from what others are doing.** Never underestimate how important it is to keep your own energy up – or how valuable it is to get ideas from other people! If you find yourself saying something like, "I'm too busy to read other people's blogs!" rethink your approach. If you thoughtfully choose content to read, you will be more productive and you'll get the time you invested back and then some.

Instagram

Have you ever wondered how you could possibly support a community on a platform that moves quickly, is focused on pictures and doesn't have any function that allows you to create groups? That's the challenge with Instagram – and here are a few solutions!

- **Use hashtags.** Hashtags are used heavily on Instagram and, in their own way, act as a way to build community. Whether people search your hashtag or click-through a hashtag on a post, the result is the same: related images that your community is probably interested in. From those hashtags, you can find people, events, and ideas your community is talking about.
- **Push content.** You might have something to share that's more easily hosted on another platform, but that doesn't mean you can't share the opportunity on Instagram! If you have an event, contest, or new product they can learn more about on your website or other social media platform, announce it on Instagram with a creative image and provide a link for more information in the description.
- **Encourage mentions.** If you're running a contest or you just have a fun community who enjoys shout-outs, encourage your community members to mention you in their posts. You can join a hashtag and/or issue a challenge and end with, "Tag @username so we can see what you're doing!"

Microblogging (Twitter, Tumblr)

In 2006, Evan Williams launched Twitter, a microblogging social media site. Many people wondered then – and still wonder today – how a site that limits individual communication to 140 characters can be used to build community. Like the techniques used on Instagram, hashtags, mentions, and directing people to other sources where they can read details can also connect your community on Twitter and help you find viable community members. Here are a few other techniques specific to Twitter you might find helpful.

- **Solve problems.** Don't just join conversations; seek out hashtags and keywords associated with problems your community can solve. Your members are likely to engage with you if the work you're doing is important to them – and you'll probably pick up a few new members along the way.
- **Host a Twitter chat.** Hosting a Twitter chat – a version of solving a problem – is one way to establish yourself as an expert and meaningful community to be a part of. People will be drawn to you by the topic of your chat, but they will stay if you demonstrate that you are knowledgeable and lead a beneficial group for them to join.
- **Tag your existing community members.** Tweets are transparent and that can work to your advantage. Tag community members as appropriate and you can automatically increase your reach and simultaneously strengthen your relationship with the community members you tagged.
- **Create lists.** When you add someone to a list, they're notified. If your list is clearly named and public, they can see your purpose and who else is on your list. This may lead to them connecting with you or others on the list – either of which increases the chances that they will become an active community member.

Facebook

Since Facebook actually has features that allow you to create and manage online groups, it is probably the most obvious option on our list. Here's an overview of how you can build and support your community through Facebook.

- **Create a private group.** Facebook allows you to quickly and easily create a Facebook group that will allow you to bring people together. Marking that group private gives a level of exclusivity that can strengthen your community! Depending on the group, a private status can also allow you to share content you may not want to be public (e.g., early drafts of materials you'd like feedback on) or deals you want to offer a select group.
- **Create a public group.** A public group can also be a great fit – especially as a way to gain visibility. Compared to a private group, the content shared is much different, but it can be equally beneficial, especially for people trying to make meaningful connections. The focus on a public community should be less about feedback and support and more about sharing ideas.
- **Create events – and share them.** If you have an event – in-person or virtual – create a Facebook event from your organization's business page. An event allows you to connect with people in different ways – inviting them to express an interest or commit to going. Whatever level of commitment they share, if they engage, you can post updates as the event approaches. It's a great setup that allows you to remain connected over a period of time – the perfect approach to building a community.
- **Look for public groups.** Not only can you create a public group, you can join them, too! You might find groups similar or complementary to yours. If you're a consulting firm that specializes in change management, your group might be focused on change management consultants. But you might find groups for organizational development trainers, change management authors, or a general group for consultants with different backgrounds that are the perfect resource for content or community members.

- **Look for pages with goals that complement your group.** You don't have to limit yourself to groups – try connecting with businesses through their pages. Remember, a good community has something to offer, so if you find a business related to your community, introduce yourself by describing what you have to offer their members.

LinkedIn

For many professionals, finding groups on LinkedIn is the obvious choice when building community. Since the platform supports professional relationships, it's the perfect place to find peers interested in content you have to share or help with questions you might have. LinkedIn does support connections through groups and you approach to both may be very similar, even if your tone on the more professional platform (LinkedIn) is slightly different.

- **Create a group.** If you feel you have a unique offering and are able to commit the time and energy needed, it's easy to create a group on LinkedIn. You can set group rules, provide a detailed description to help attract members who would benefit most, and control the application process – allowing everyone to join immediately or requiring new members to be accepted. From there, you can add content and comment on what others have shared to ensure the group is valuable.
- **Join a group.** Don't underestimate the value of joining a group and becoming an active member. Often times people view their message as so unique, they have to *create* a place to discuss the content and ideas when, in actuality, there are a lot of groups that already exist – people who have already gathered – who would be very interested in what you have to share. It's less work for you and you already have an engaged audience so you can get your message up and running faster.

- **Create and maintain your company page.** Groups are about bringing people together and, if you represent an organization, your supporters will happily connect through your company page. Once you've crafted your page, you can keep followers interested by posting updates that will help them – not just updates about your organization.
- **Engage on other company pages.** Like groups, remember that you don't have generate all of the messages – you can engage with others on their pages. Look for companies that complement your business. For example, if you run a medical device company, you could potentially make connections with companies doing medical research.

Considerations for Every Platform

Wherever your community engages with you, there are several facts you can count on and techniques you can use to maximize your effectiveness.

- Your community will likely engage some or all of the time from a mobile device. Make your content mobile compatible!
- For every ask, think about how much you've given. Don't ask too much of your community or they will slowly abandon you.
- Hashtags are used to varying degrees on different platforms. Understand how they are used on each platform and follow the rules.
- Make it easy to engage and share. The more your community members have to do, the less likely they are to stay connected.

Chapter 8 Discussion

1. Create an editorial calendar or add community engagement opportunities to your existing planning system. Include holidays, events, popular hashtags within your community, and any other possible conversation starters.

2. Of the engagement tactics listed in this chapter, which ideas do you think would work best in your community? Why?

Part Four

Make the Best of Every Situation

Chapter 9

Guidelines for Managing a Social Media Community

A social media manager is responsible for multiple aspects of an organization's online presence.

- Content creation/sharing
- Responding to positive and negative feedback
- Surveying the community (formally and informally)
- Maintaining relationships in the community

Each of these steps has layers of complexity and – especially when considering all of the unknowns – they can be intimidating. But as we've seen in this book and several of the other NISM books, agreeing on goals and best practices can make even the most challenging situations easier to handle.

In this section of the book, we're going to look at some of the more difficult situations community managers face. In any community – a small or large business, a nonprofit, or an interest group – there is a risk that you as the community manager will encounter challenging people and situations. We'll outline how a community manager can create guidelines to help manage those challenges when they arise.

Posting Community Guidelines

Most online platforms allow the community manager to limit posting rights if necessary, but it's important to remember the trade-off associated with limiting how community members are allowed to participate. For example, if all comments have to be approved before they appear on a blog post, there will be at best a short delay before a community member's post becomes visible. This may leave the community member feeling like they are being censored. It might also decrease chatter simply because it takes longer for content to appear that other members might respond to.

Whether or not a community manager chooses to allow members to post without restrictions, a clear policy for posting should always be available. The guidelines should include what content is acceptable for posting and how violations of the posting policy will be managed (e.g., posts will be removed, after 2 infractions offenders will be removed from the group, etc.). The policy should have a professional tone and clearly state what is and isn't acceptable.

Options for Community Guidelines

If you're still not quite sure what a fair list of community guidelines might look like, check the following list. When considering your own community, some of these may not seem relevant. You might find that others need an adjustment to work for you. If those are the thoughts going through your mind, you're doing the right thing. Guidelines should be adjusted for every community, but hopefully these ideas will at least get you started. It's unlikely anyone would use all of these posts – especially since some overlap – but the wide variety of options should be enough to help you write guidelines that represent your community.

Warn people about what posts will be deleted related to language or intent.

Hate speech will be deleted. This includes, but is not limited to, disparaging remarks or negative generalizations made related to gender, sexual orientation, gender identity, race, religion, or national origin.

Any personal attacks or threats against the writer or another commenter will be deleted. Phrases like "your kind" or "you're the kind of person who" are flagged, no matter what side you're on.

Negative "jokes" or comments about physical characteristics of a person will be deleted. This includes references to the writers, commenters, celebrities, and groups of people.

Any content posted by a person claiming to be someone they are not, or representing an organization they are not affiliated with will be deleted.

Any post the moderator determines was intended to anger other community members or start a fight will be deleted – no matter what side you're on.

Warn people about what posts will be deleted related to content.

Any reference to illegal activity or suggestions – even in jest – for breaking the law will be deleted.

Plagiarized content and any material found to be in violation of copyright law will be deleted.

Unless previously approved, no advertising or fundraising is permitted and will be deleted.

Comments that make it clear that you did not view the content will be deleted.

Clearly state what will get people banned.

If the moderator has to delete your comment twice for the same reason, your account is at risk of being banned. A third violation will automatically result in a ban.

If you are new to the community and seem to have joined just to contribute hateful remarks, a single violation will lead to a ban from the site. The absence of a history with the group indicates that you are a troll, and to ensure the community continues to be a safe place for people to connect with others, we will implement a zero-tolerance policy.

It is at the moderator's discretion to ban anyone they determine to be detrimental to the group for any reason and without warning.

Tell people what kind of content you'd like to see.

Challenge our thinking, but stick to the facts. Personal attacks will be deleted, but we welcome fact-based comments that challenge what we have to say.

If you see a comment that is inappropriate, please let us know. We value your opinion and welcome your support in monitoring these discussions. However, we do ask that you not engage with anyone who has posted inflammatory comments (this is known as "feeding the trolls") as it only encourages their negative behavior.

If you see an error (content, typo, etc.), please let us know!

A comment that would get you banned from one community may be perfectly acceptable to another. That doesn't mean either community is better or worse – it means the community managers have chosen how to best support their communities and the results are different. The most important thing for community managers to do is clearly articulate community guidelines and enforce them consistently.

You might also add unique community participation guidelines like language restrictions or citation requirements for facts referenced – it is up to you! Just remember that you don't want so many guidelines that it's difficult for people to participate, but you don't want so few that your community members don't feel comfortable participating.

Steps to Follow to Resolve an Issue Online

A few years ago, I decided to put Comcast to the test. I had been having trouble for a few months with my cable service. I was also teaching a social media marketing class at the time and I realized I had the opportunity to demonstrate the opportunities an organization might have by handling a customer concern through a social media platform.

In order to do well, I explained to my class that Comcast would need to do the following things:

- Respond quickly to my concern
- Figure out why I was upset
- Apologize
- Identify a solution
- Connect me with the person who could resolve the issue I was having

With each of these criteria in mind, here's what happened:

Respond quickly.

I sent a tweet to @comcastcares and received a response from a customer service representative in 43 seconds. That was an impressive response time.

In my tweet, I said that I had outlined the challenges I was having in a Tumblr post and I shared the link. (I wasn't trying to be dramatic or integrate another platform; it was just genuinely a long story and Tumblr was the best place I could think of to write it.) The representative who tweeted at me didn't acknowledge my blog post – in fact, I briefly wondered if he noticed that I referenced it.

Interpret why the customer is angry.

The representative shared an email address and asked me to send him the details of what was wrong with my cable service. I was momentarily irritated because I had written everything out already and I did tell him where he could find the details – I assumed he hadn't read my tweet. In hindsight, I realized he was likely following protocol and it was brilliant! He had an upset customer expressing her grievances on a public platform. What was the first thing he did? While expressing concern and offering to help, he was moving me from a public platform to a private communication method.

Identify a solution.

I emailed my concerns as I was instructed and the next day I was contacted by a customer service representative. She asked me a few additional questions, explained what she could see in her system about the issues I was having, and then scheduled a time for a technician to come out.

Apologize if you do something wrong.

The original customer service representative apologized in a tweet. The woman who eventually resolved my issue apologized twice. Both seemed genuine and were meaningful, though I have to admit the ones from the woman resolving my issue were more meaningful. Upon reflection, I realized it was because the tweet was more like a requirement – a knee-jerk reaction. It was still the right thing to do, but how sorry could he really be when he knew nothing about what had happened? I originally thought I appreciated the second apology more because she had actually taken steps to fix the problem I had, but eventually I realized it was because it was more sincere. She could see what had happened and only she could genuinely acknowledge that I had a bad experience.

Connect the customer to the right person in the organization.

I had been working with the customer service department for months. At the time, I lived in an area that had spotty coverage and I didn't have any other option for service. With each call, I talked to another customer service representative who apologized and sent another technician. The representative I connected with through Twitter took a completely different approach and resolved my issue in just a few days. Was it a coincidence? Or does Comcast route their high-profile complaints (i.e., anything on social media) to more experienced employees? I asked and never got an answer, but if they did, I would have to agree that it's a smart approach. From a reputation management standpoint, it's important to keep as many of the people who are active on social media happy as you can.

Why was Comcast able to resolve my issue so successfully?

Comcast clearly had a plan for responding to upset customers. If you consider my story, you can see the perfect delivery that ended up transforming me from someone complaining on a public platform to a happy customer.

- **Responded quickly to my concern** – and, taking it a step further, moved me from a public platform. If this isn't their policy, it should be – it was executed seamlessly.
- **Figured out why I was upset.** The initial representative learned enough to know where to direct my concern and the second knew enough to resolve it. They each understood their role.
- **Apologize.** Each representative apologized. Though they had different perspectives, both were appreciated. I am sure an apology is part of the script, but my experience reminded me that even scripted apologies can be sincere. As a side note, in this particular situation I had felt like previous representatives didn't believe I was having the issues I was having. Had they not apologized, those feelings would have likely returned and I would have felt even more upset.
- **Identify a solution.** There were multiple solutions identified. I was routed to the correct representative and she eventually resolved my issue. She had to research information and coordinate field team members. The entire team did very well.
- **Connect me with the person who could resolve the issue I was having.** Again, this happened at several stages, as is often the case when resolving a customer concern. Rarely can one person solve every issue within an organization, but an informed and organized team

can efficiently route their customers to the people who can help them.

What customer concerns might emerge within your community? Do you have a system in place to manage them efficiently? Fear of the unknown can intimidate community managers, but it doesn't have to. Simply create a decision tree that will work specifically for your organization. Once you fill in each of the blanks – getting help from others in your organization – you can approach any customer concern with confidence.

Getting Started

Some people seem to have a gift for resolving issues, calming people who are upset, and helping people open up and share their concerns. The rest of us have to *learn techniques*. So where do we start?

The following is a decision tree – and it is simplified. Rarely do we ever have customers who are complaining or complimenting us fully. It's very common to hear:

"The manager at your Pineview location is doing the best she can, but you have got to staff that place better. I waited more than an hour!"

"I have been a loyal customer for 10 years – I haven't complained once! But this was too much. If you're going to send service reps out that late, we'll find another provider."

"I just wanted to call and compliment Jake. He does an awesome job getting my car serviced quickly – and he's so nice! The poor guy is constantly training new people, but he never lets it affect service."

How would those calls, comments, emails, etc. be routed? My guess is that the first comment would register as a complaint and the Pineview manager would never hear that someone out there recognized her hard work. The second would probably be a complaint, too – we'd likely overlook the fact that we did something right for 10 years! And the third might register as a compliment, but critical information about staff turnover is shared. We're glad Jake does well, but we need to figure out why he has to keep hiring new staff.

Eventually, you can grow your customer response team to get the customer to the right place and all of the right information to the individuals who need it. To start, you have to teach people the basics of what to do when. If employees handling customer feedback don't understand what to do when, they're more likely to panic, make a mistake, not respond at all, or quit! Start your conversation with them by providing a basic outline like this to help them manage feedback.

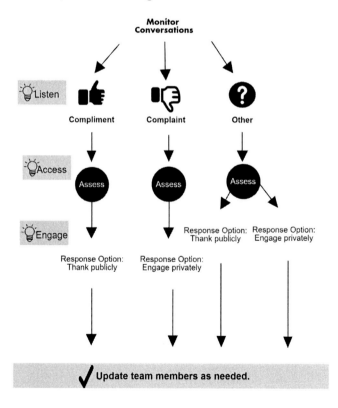

Compliments

Especially when we're busy, we often miss the opportunity to assess positive feedback and then publicly thank the sender. This is a missed opportunity! Not only does thanking the happy customer strengthen our relationship, it's also an opportunity to keep a positive conversation going and increase the chances that more people will see it.

Complaints

The goal of a complaint online is always to move it to a private platform. Invite the customer to call a special number or email the details. Acknowledge their concerns and provide them with a private outlet.

The Unknown

What if your conversation is both a compliment and a complaint? Or it starts out as one and then turns into another? Don't worry – you can apply the exact same tools and route the information to a solution as needed. Use common sense – if someone is 90% upset, don't share their feedback and acknowledge the 10% of the post that's a compliment. But you might elect to pass the positive feedback on to the people directly involved.

The benefit of a simple chart like this is that it helps everyone carry out the good decisions they're already capable of making. The structure can boost confidence and help everyone remember to capitalize on the opportunities that are available.

Chapter 9 Discussion

1. Search for two recent examples of unhappy customers expressing concerns on social media – one that was handled well and one that was handled poorly. For each organization, answer the following questions.

   a. Complete light research to learn more about each organization. How large are they? On what platforms do they engage with their customers?

   b. Does the organization appear to use a personal, corporate, or response community persona?

   c. Whether the overall situation was handled well or poorly, identify one thing that was done well and one thing that could have been done better.

2. Create or update the guidelines for your community. What potential additions are relevant to your community?

Part Five
The SMS Exam

Chapter 10

What Do You Need to Know for the SMS Exam?

I f you're reading this book, there's a chance you're preparing to take the certified SMS exam. This section presents the key topics you can expect to encounter during the exam – but even if you aren't taking the exam, the following section is a good review of some of the highlights of what's covered in this book. Review the following list and refer back to the text or to external resources as needed to ensure you thoroughly understand each topic.

How would you use an editorial calendar as a community manager?

Most people think of using an editorial calendar for scheduling content, but it can be used to organize your communication with your community as well. As a community manager, you might think of something that will work for your specific community, but here is a recap of a few general uses:

- **Add routine communication to your calendar.** You know your community, events that are important, and when they are most likely to be online. Be sure to catch those key times for 2-way conversations by adding them to your calendar.
- **Pre-plan some of your engagement questions.** Don't give up off-the-cuff responses, but have questions

ready in case you're short on time or are struggling to think of a post in real-time.

- **Highlight when your community is most active on which platforms.** Focus on the platforms most likely to have conversations you should join. Also, keep an eye out for key members of the community you should engage with during these conversations.
- **Note any events related to your community that you'll attend or engage with in real-time.** Include hashtags, key people to follow, links to the event information, and any other critical information that will help you engage fully in the event.
- **Link your calendar to additional resources.** Create a shared folder with images or a document with content that works well with the potential community engagement you've identified.

Have two-way conversations with customers on social media platforms.

As a community manager, you're responsible for publishing content and more! It's critical to engage your audience in two-way conversations. You might ask questions, respond to comments, or share material that sparks a conversation online. Focus on adding value to your community by talking with community members, not just at them!

How can you reach out and engage with your audience on a frequent basis?

An effective community manager will spend a lot of their time reacting to opportunities that come their way. Varied and frequent activity is always the goal, and the easiest way to achieve that goal is by responding to opportunities as they present themselves in your community.

Make connections between community members.

You might facilitate a formal introduction or tag someone saying, "Jolene, you should check out Z a - hir's post. I think your insights would be valuable."

Read, comment, and respond to the content or comments of your customers.

For every ten posts you share, you might have one that really strikes a chord with your community. Follow their lead! If they find the content funny, interesting, or have questions, do what you can to keep the conversation going. You're better off focusing your energy on content that's proving to be interesting than by trying to revive content your community has passed on – unless something outside your platform happens to generate new interest.

Recognize accomplishments of those in your network.

Your community members are doing all kinds of amazing things in the world. Do you have a way to keep track of and then acknowledge them? Set up systems to identify keywords and names and – however you come across the accomplishments of your community – acknowledge them publicly.

Develop a plan to manage unhappy community members.

One of the most daunting tasks a community faces is how to manage an unhappy person who has expressed their discontent on a public platform. But as we learned, a good plan can leave you prepared for anything – just follow these steps:

- *Respond quickly.*
- *Interpret why the customer is angry.*

- *Identify a solution.*
- *Apologize if you do something wrong.*
- *Connect the customer to the right person in the organization.*

And most importantly, empathize with your audience. Look beyond the words and attempt to understand what is really bothering the customer.

Additional Resources

Excerpt about community building from the original NISM textbook:

By developing a personality and maintaining a consistent voice, you will put your organization in a position to get likes and grow its audience. In this topic, leverage your social media community management to build relationships that, in turn, will help your organization's audience grow and increase the positive reception of your brand and social media activities.

Relationship Building in a Digital Environment

In the social media world, relationships are formed and measured in a variety of ways, depending on the social media platform being used. For example, on microblogs like Twitter, you have a relationship with those you follow and those who follow you. The same can be said for people who like your company page on social networks such as Facebook, and those who share and link back to your blog. One thing to remember is that you can buy likes and followers, but simply having a "like" does not translate into a true lasting relationship between an organization and its social media community.

Your organization should be trying to win real fans and followers. The more people your organization has a relationship with, the more reach it has through social media in terms of direct relationships. It also has more potential reach in terms of accessing the friends of your fans. The more reach your organization has, the more powerful its social media presence. With real reach, more advocates will rise up for your brand, and the more impact your social media presence can have. This applies to everything from lead generation to getting its message out to the public.

Winning Friends and Influencing People in Social Media

The book How to Win Friends and Influence People *was written by Dale Carnegie and published in 1936. In the book, Carnegie advocated that many people need of a course solely on how to get along with other people. This book is one of the world's best-selling guides on how to successfully build productive business relationships. The principles in the book are still true today and translate well into the digital world. In fact, the book has been updated and a new version,* How to Win Friends and Influence People in the Digital Age, *was published in 2012.*

In social media, you should be trying to elevate your approach to establish and build relationships. Using social media as a one-to-many broadcast system is not the most effective way to increase your reach and build brand advocates. As a social media strategist, you should think about how the key principles of relationship building translate to social media, and use those principles to build your social media relationships and community following.

Show Genuine Interest

Show genuine interest in other people. Remember it's recommended that organizations spend 80 percent of their time listening on social media. Through social listening, you can give your community your attention and respond, when needs or concerns arise. You can also solicit feedback from your community by asking questions. Social listening is the first step. You can show interest in something that was said in many ways through social media by liking something, commenting on it, retweeting it, sharing it, linking back to the source, and so forth. These types of actions show that your organization is paying attention and that you are interested and care. It makes others feel good when they see your response.

Show Honest and Sincere Appreciation

In an interpersonal relationship, appreciation might take the form of a compliment, a thank you, a congratulations, or an atta-boy. In the digital world, reach out to those that recognize you and say thank you. Say thank you for actions such as sharing, following, retweeting, liking, or commenting. Post recommendations on LinkedIn for those people who are deserving of it. Take notice of people who notice you and show appreciation.

Arouse Interest Through Storytelling

Organizations use social media to arouse interest in the products and services they have to offer. As a social media strategist, you want your community to care about what your organization has to offer and to buy its products or services. A good way to get your audience to care is through storytelling. Stories are how we frame our history, and how we consume the content we enjoy in the form of books, shows, and movies. It's a way we all like to process information and a great way to explain what your organization has to offer.

Stories should have a beginning, a middle, and end. The beginning should frame the issue you wish to address. The middle should show how to resolve the issue, perhaps through the use of products or services you're offering. The end should sum up the expected outcome and show benefits. Most people don't sell their services through storytelling. Most use a one-to-many broadcast approach. For example, a realtor who comes to a buyers meeting and says, "I have homes for sale," is broadcasting. The realtor is not providing a full story. A better approach might be that he says he has homes for sale (the beginning). Then he might go on to say that he knows the area very well, including all the different styles of homes, and that all people have to do is contact him (the middle). Then he should describe the outcome that his audience will want to hear by telling them they will find the perfect home (the end).

Storytelling is more thoughtful and engaging than broadcasting, and it taps into the comfortable way in which most people like to process information. It allows you to state your value proposition and advocate for yourself without appearing arrogant. Since many other people will be broadcasting rather than storytelling, there is a good chance your message will rise above the white noise that abounds in social media.

Encourage Others to Share About Themselves

A great way to show interest and learn about your community is to encourage your community members to share about themselves. If you can get members of your community sharing, you can listen for how your products or services have been helpful, where problems have arisen, and learn what your community thinks of your brand. You can encourage people to share by asking direct questions such as, "How do you primarily use our product." You can also ask your community to share their favorite stories. For example, if an organization is about to celebrate its 10th anniversary, you might ask the social media community to share their favorite stories from the past decade related to the organization, and its products or services.

Speak to Other Parties' Interests

Where interests are shared, it's easy to communicate. When interests diverge, communication become more difficult. But in social media, and interpersonally, it's often of value to try to communicate with individuals who have diverging interests or opinions. If you *can't find common ground on your terms, then explore theirs. It's very easy to speak to the other parties' interests; simply ask them questions about their interests. Ask them what they are interested in the topic, how they got interested in it, who shares in their interest, and so forth. You can discover a lot by speaking to other people's interests. Not only will this show that you are interested in them, you may also find patterns in your community that can lead you to identify new market segments or innovations in your products or services.*

Make Others Feel Important

It's important to make others feel important. Showing interest and appreciation will help to make members of your community feel that they are important. If members of your community feel important, they will be more active, and they will be more likely to advocate for your brand. When they do that, they spread your brand message to people they know, potentially increasing your reach. You can make members of your community feel important through your interactions, by commenting on their posts, acknowledging good points, and responding to their customer service needs.

You can also give members of your community responsibilities. You can ask them to comment on certain types of posts, provide feedback in other ways, provide guest posts, be the subject of an interview, or provide feedback on how your products and services can be better. Essentially, ask them to help you. This type of interaction not only makes them feel important, it also provides good information to you and your organization, and it builds trust within the social media community.

Glossary of Terms

Advocate
An individual who talks about a brand in a supportive or positive manner, on their personal social media platforms.

Audience
Anyone receiving the information an organization is sharing.

Community
People who are regularly engaged with your digital presence.

Community Management
The process of ensuring that the two-way online communication between the organization and its customers always flows smoothly.

Editorial Calendar
Tool that organizes the process of creating and publishing content, as well as noting opportunities to engage with others during events.

Evangelist
A community member who emphatically promotes your community and its message.

Loafer
Someone who has always been or recently became inactive within your community.

Real-Time Marketing
Brand promotion through conversations surrounding current trends and topics.

Social Listening
Continuous monitoring of online conversations to better understand customer wants and needs. Also called *social monitoring*.

Social Persona
An image you create and use online to advocate for a brand or represent an organization. It is similar to the role an actor would play.

#TBT
Popular hashtag meaning "throwback Thursday" used by people posting old pictures or posts on Thursday.

Troll
Individual who looks for opportunities to start arguments and cause trouble online.